A Teachable Spirit

*Guidelines for starting Bible studies for women,
from someone who did*

A Teachable Spirit

by

Paulette Woods

Guidelines for starting Bible studies for women,
from someone who did

Beacon Hill Press of Kansas City
Kansas City, Missouri

Copyright 1984

by Beacon Hill Press of Kansas City
Printed in the United States of America

ISBN: 0-8341-0904-2

Cover art: Crandall Vail

Permission to quote from the following copyrighted version of the Bible is acknowledged with appreciation:

The Holy Bible, New International Version (NIV), copyright © 1978 by the New York International Bible Society.

10 9 8 7 6 5 4 3 2

This book is dedicated to Ruth Barnes,
my darling mother—
the woman who has the most teachable spirit
I've ever known.

Contents

Prologue

Here I sit on the concrete at my front door—locked out. I can't believe that just minutes ago I was having a lovely luncheon with people that I love, and now—I'm locked out of my own house.

It happened so easily. You see, Jonathan's home from school, so I no longer have a car. I get escorted places and dropped. I bum rides with friends or even strangers. I've wondered about those people hitchhiking; probably they have a son home from college and they were dropped off.

We now share one car, one set of car keys, and one house key, so he took me to the luncheon. I said, "If you leave how will I get in?" His famous last words were, "Oh, don't worry, Mom, I'll put the house key in our spot; you just catch a ride home and go right in."

There's just one tiny problem: he forgot to put the house key in our spot. I can see my comfortable chairs; the rent is paid; I really do live here. But I can't get in.

There was a time in my spiritual life like this. The price had been paid; I was with precious people; I could see the neat things that God did for them; I even sensed the excitement. But I felt locked out. Dumb, I know, but you see, commitment to Jesus is the key. My relationship with Him on a daily basis opens the door to my real world. He makes me comfortable with others who are secure and growing. It's not enough to peer in the windows and wish I were inside; with Him I go right on in. With Him we are never locked out. He wants us to be fulfilled and happy. This comes to full fruition when we begin to pour our lives into others.

My life has been so blessed by the teaching of others. Much time and love has been poured into me, and I am grateful. The only way I can repay the debt is to share with others in the same measure.

A Teachable Spirit is the story of how God brought me to the place where I could be taught and in turn learn how to teach others. Please know that I'm not an authority. Most of the time I'm just a little girl inside—unsure and still learning; but one thing I know: Jesus loves me and I want to share it.

With all my heart I want this book to spark your ability or rather availability to share Jesus with women through Bible study.

So many people are hungry for the Word simply given. You don't have to be profound or eloquent. Just be yourself, it is enough.

There is a gentleness in Christian women that responds to the needs of others. Oh, how our world needs your gentleness! Please believe that you can be used of God. Your life is precious to Jesus, but the perfume must get out of the bottle if others are to share the fragrance.

The longer I live the more I know it's the simple things in life that really matter. A Bible study may seem so simple that you've overlooked the potential. It was my place to bloom where planted, and it is yours, as well.

You have the tools: Jesus, you, the Word, your home, and friends. Get going, you can do it . . . because you have "a teachable spirit."

1

A Teachable Spirit

The aged women likewise, that they be in behaviour as becometh *holiness,* not false accusers, not given to much wine, teachers of good things; that they may teach the young women to be sober, to love their husbands, to love their children, to be discreet, chaste, keepers at home, good, obedient to their own husbands, that the word of God be not blasphemed.   *Titus 2:3-5, italics added*

God cannot use an uncommitted life. Until I was willing to submit to the control of the Holy Spirit, my life was lived in vain.

In order to teach, we must first be taught of the Holy Spirit, and we cannot be taught until we are surrendered to His will for our lives. We simply do not receive the messages He gives out.

The infilling of the Holy Spirit is vital to leadership. You must be surrendered to the Lordship of Jesus Christ, or you will teach in the flesh and it will only be an ego trip for you. The Word declares, "The letter killeth, but the spirit giveth life" (2 Cor. 3:6).

I grew up in a parsonage and all my father's sermons seemed to be on holiness. I resented the teaching and would say, "Daddy, why can't God do it all at once? Isn't that possible?" Being strong-willed and stubborn, I would just tune that part of his sermons out. It's amazing what we can will ourselves to hear or not hear.

I couldn't get established in the Lord. I was a chronic seeker.

Every revival, Dad could count on one getting saved—me. I would set out with such high enthusiasm. Just one thing was lacking: *Commitment.*

Living in a parsonage in the '50s was an interesting experience; it was like living in a goldfish bowl. Everyone knew every move I made. When I did something they disapproved of, they usually felt led to inform my parents. I resented their intrusion into my life.

I graduated from high school and went away to college possessing a trunk of hand-me-down clothes and a hand-me-down religion. We had devotions around the breakfast table. Dad read the Bible and Bertha Munro's *Truth for Today.* Each evening we had family prayer time. I have vivid pictures of us kneeling in the living room of that little parsonage in Cairo. I guess I thought Daddy's prayers would get me through. Oh, I had read the Bible and prayed, but only as a duty. I didn't love to do it.

Trevecca Nazarene College struck me as a perpetual youth camp. Surely I'll make it here, I thought. But I didn't count on one thing. *I* came along with the trunk of hand-me-down religion.

When Gerald and I started going together, I sighed with relief. "Here is a strong person! I can depend on him to see me through." He loved Jesus so much, and he was *committed.* He even wanted to go to the mission field. That frightened me! I didn't want to live in a glass house, much less a mud hut. But Gerald is such a beautiful person I stuck with him. Then he told me God had called him to pastor. I nearly died. But right away I decided, I'll do it. I was genuine plastic.

I believed in the tooth fairy and other such nonsense. I had even swallowed the line, "And they lived happily ever after." I was able to carry it off for the first seven years. Then my carriage turned back into a pumpkin, and there I was in a parsonage scrubbing ugly blue tile. My Prince Charming had mounted his white steed and ridden off to his parish. There I was, stuck with two babies, a phone that rang all the time, and ugly blue tile that went with the house that the prince expected *me* to keep perfect . . . oh, yuck!

I hated everything, especially me! My form of religion had let me down! I was depressed and lonely. I felt everyone had a life but me. I thought, "What's a nice girl like me doing in a place like this?"

Each year in November, we went to a pastors and wives' retreat at Sumatanga, a Methodist lodge in north Alabama. That year, since we lived so close, we were the host pastor and wife. We arrived early to prepare the guest rooms and register the couples as they came in.

Mrs. Reeford Chaney, our district superintendent's wife, asked if I would also go by and escort Mrs. Audrey Williamson to our ladies' sessions.

What a love! Mrs. Williamson snuggled up to me as we walked together, and I felt warmed for the first time in an age. When she stood and quoted Isaiah 55, I felt the door of my heart swing open. Oh, how the Word of God pierced my soul! I was so *thirsty*. The Lord said, "Come . . . and I will make an everlasting covenant with you, even the sure mercies of David" (v. 3). My heart cried out, "O Father, would You forgive my rebellious, stubborn spirit even as You forgave David?"

Dr. Williamson gave an invitation that morning and I was truly a seeker. Jesus came and forgave me, and I became a born-again believer that day. After the retreat I hungered for the Word and longed for the fullness of His Spirit. Everyday I pored over the Bible and the old hymns. I wrote as I read. I couldn't believe the thoughts that poured out of my spirit. We were made to fellowship with God, and I was experiencing it.

In February we went to an indoor camp meeting in Birmingham. Dr. Edward Lawlor was the speaker, and as he spoke my heart cried out for what was being offered. I couldn't wait for the invitation to be given. As I walked to the altar, the devil said, "What a fool you're making of yourself, here in front of your husband's peers." Almost aloud I said, "I'm sick of what people think and say. I just want to hear what God has to say." As I knelt, my heart thumped so loud I just knew everyone heard it. My friends came to pray with me, and they told me how nice I was, but I knew and God knew what a phony I had been. No more indecision. I told God, "I want all You have for me. I want to die to my will and way; I want to love You above all else. Change my attitude, and please, Jesus, put a love for the pastorate in my heart. Cleanse me, O God, without, within."

Nothing happened that night. It was as though I had surrendered without the sweetness of victory—back home and back into the Word.

For as the rain cometh down, and the snow from heaven, and returneth not thither, but watereth the earth, and maketh it bring forth and bud, and it may give seed to the sower, and bread to the eater: so shall my word be that goeth forth out of my mouth: it shall not return unto me void, but it shall accomplish that which

I please, and it shall prosper in the thing whereto I sent it. For ye shall go out with joy, and be led forth with peace: the mountains and the hills shall break forth before you into singing, and all the trees of the field shall clap their hands. Instead of the thorn shall come up the fir tree, and instead of the brier shall come up the myrtle tree: and it shall be to the Lord for a name, for an everlasting sign that shall not be cut off *(Isa. 55:10-13)*.

About two weeks later I was back mopping that ugly blue tile when the glory began to fall. The last door had opened and I could finally trust all the unknown to the Lord. He kept saying, "I can handle it; you'll love *My* way." And do you know, I have!

That day He put such a love for His people in my heart. When I would walk down the streets of that town, I wanted to gather people in my arms and tell them, "Jesus loves you so much, and so do I."

What a changed person I was! Gerald's parish became mine. His singleness of purpose, to win the lost, became mine, too. I belonged! And at long last I was free to be me, the Paulette that God had made, not the one shaped by people's opinions and judgments. I was finally free, free to be the person God dreamed I could be. Oh, what a difference! He changed me!

The word "sanctified" became a new word for me. I finally knew what it meant: a right relationship with God, a vessel, clean and ready for the Master's use. "An everlasting sign that shall not be cut off"—His love in me.

Before I had nothing to say. Now I was ready to teach. He would do the teaching, now that I had *a teachable spirit.*

The basic tools for teaching are a committed life and the Word of God. Seek His will to be a successful Bible study teacher. You can because He will!

Bible Study

A Teachable Spirit

1. But the _____, which is the _____
   _____, whom the Father will send in my name, he
   shall _____ you all things, and bring all things to

14

your _____, whatsoever I have said unto you (John 14:26).

2. Which things also we _____, not in the words which man's _____ _____, but which the _____ _____ teacheth; comparing _____ _____ with spiritual (1 Cor. 2:13).

3. But when they shall lead you, and deliver you up, take no thought _____ what ye shall _____, neither do ye premeditate: but whatsoever shall _____ _____ _____ in that hour, that _____ ye: for it is not _____ that _____, but the _____ _____ (Mark 13:11).

4. For the _____ _____ shall _____ you in the same hour what ye ought to _____ (Luke 12:12).

5. Take heed therefore unto _____, and to all the _____, over the which the _____ _____ hath made you _____, to _____ the church of God, which he hath _____ with his own _____ (Acts 20:28).

6. Giving no _____ in any thing, that the _____ be not blamed (2 Cor. 6:3). By _____, by _____, by _____, by _____, by the _____ _____, by _____ _____ (2 Cor. 6:6).

7. For our _____ came not unto you in _____ only, but also in _____, and in the _____ _____, and in much _____; as ye know what manner of _____ we were among you for _____ _____ (1 Thess. 1:5).

8. Unto whom it was _____, that not unto

_____, but unto us they did

_____ the things, which are now

_____ unto you by them that have

_____ the gospel unto you with the

_____ _____ sent down from _____;

which things the _____ desire to look into (1 Pet. 1:12).

This study is to help you see who the Teacher really is. In Acts 1:8 we read, "But ye shall receive power, after that the Holy Ghost is come upon you." My longing for you is that you will tarry for the power. It is your inheritance. The Holy Spirit is for you today!

2

Ola and Me

When Ola came into my life she was 70, and I was 23. Neither of us noticed the age difference. I did notice that she wore funny shoes, but I adored her and she loved me. Thus began our friendship.

She was strong-willed and opinionated. She told me I should let my hair grow out and wear it on top my head so I would appear more godly. My hair was very short. She thought I wasted potatoes, so she bought me a potato peeler. In spite of these shortcomings she saw potential in me and began to pour her life into mine; we became family.

I'm sure she weighed all of 90 pounds, but that 90 pounds was sheer dynamite. It's fair to say she was pushy, but the Lord sent her to me. No one else could see my need the way she could. I know she knew that I was lost, while others didn't seem to even notice that I had a problem. God uses unusual people to get our attention. Ola was certainly not ordinary, and she had my attention.

Ola, a woman of the Word and of prayer, met with Jesus for her quiet time every morning, and then she would call me and share what God had shared with her. Not only did she read to me over the phone; she would sing, too.

Life for me at that time was a struggle. I had two small children and lived in a parsonage that wasn't two feet away from the church.

You could slap the front door by reaching out our bedroom window. Needless to say, my husband and I never left our work. I was frustrated and angry because I didn't want to be a pastor's wife and live in a glass house. I wasn't communicating with the Lord very well, much less with anyone else. However, Ola paid no attention. She just kept sharing with me what she was receiving from Jesus.

One of her favorite verses was "This is the day which the Lord hath made; we will rejoice and be glad in it" (Ps. 118:24). I couldn't believe the Lord had anything to do with my day. Alabama in the winter is rain—lots of it. We didn't have a dryer so I would stand in ankle-deep water to hang out my babies' diapers. They rarely got dry. Most days they ended up drying on a rack over the furnace. Gerald was in love with his work, but I was not. I was stuck in a parsonage with two babies, so lonely for Jesus, but too stubborn to cry out to Him. Oh, how I needed Him to be my dearest Friend!

Luke 17:10 reads, "When ye shall have done all those things which are commanded you, say, We are unprofitable servants: we have done that which was our duty to do." I did my duty—all the outward appearances seemed so important. I went to church each time the doors were open, served on committees, entertained, listened to problems, because it was expected of me, the pastor's wife. But oh, how dry my soul!

When I made a full surrender of my life to the Lord, I understood Ola. He put such a hunger for the Word in my heart; I would just pore over the pages, drinking it in. Words stood out in bold type. I never dreamed I could feel so alive. Every morning I would come to my quiet place and He would always meet me there. Some days were quiet, some were drenched in praise and uplift, sometimes were even a bit dry. But the daily meeting with Jesus began a process in my heart that has transformed my life from drab to full color—praise His lovely name!

I can still hear Ola say, "I will lift up mine eyes unto the hills, from whence cometh my help. My help cometh from the Lord" (Ps. 121:1-2). Suddenly I saw my life as a pastor's wife in a different light. What had been hard became a challenge. For the first time I became creative with my life. Even hanging up diapers was different. Oh, the water was still there, and the parsonage was still next door to the church, but I was changed. My attitude had a complete overhaul. The words of Jesus became a reality. "Behold, the kingdom of God is within you" (Luke 17:21). He was my Help, and as I looked to Him daily, His kingdom was coming in me. Wow!

Ola never talked about my problems; she just kept feeding me answers. She was always positive and kind, and she prayed for me. As a result of her prayers I came to know Jesus in just as personal a way as she. Ola was my friend; she taught me, through sharing what God had already taught her . . . What a friend! May God bless her.

I wanted that quiet time with the Lord, and I found it. What a blessing that personal Bible study has been through the years!

3

A Personal
Quiet Time

Examine me, O Lord, and prove me; try my reins and my
heart.   *Ps. 26:2*

When Gerald and I decided we would get up
at 6 a.m. for our quiet time, wow, I felt *so spiritual!* The plan was for
him to go to the church for his devotions, and my place would be the
sofa in the den. We had read a wonderful article about a surgeon
with a very busy schedule who took time to pray one hour every
morning. That meant getting up very early, since surgery started before most folk think about getting up. He had his quiet time even
when he was in military service, living in barracks with a lot of
guys. We were so inspired and felt surely this would be great for us.
And it was and has been through the years.

But there had to be a first morning. I was there in the den, up an
hour earlier than I'd ever been in my life. I read my Bible, prayed for
everyone I could think of, walked into the kitchen to check the time,
and had 45 minutes left to go. I went back, got on my knees to pray
some more, and went sound asleep in Zion. I woke up just before
time for Gerald to come in the door. I felt so guilty. I surely didn't
want him to know that I couldn't tarry for one hour.

I suppose I thought I would impress God by the length of my
time with Him, but He can't be impressed. He just wanted me to love
Him enough to come and share everything with Him. Another plan
was developing in my head. I would get up, make coffee, even light

a fire to make for a cozy time—anything to keep me awake. I also learned that I needed to do more than read if I was going to retain the Word. I bought a little notebook and began to write as I read. I made a prayer list and began to pray in particular for people and things. I prayed for myself, too, that God would reveal any hurtful way in me.

My prayer notebook has been a big help to me. Mine is a 7" x 9" ring binder you can pick up at any office supply counter. Dividers are also available. I use the dividers to separate the sections, and on these dividers write praise scriptures that speak to my heart. I have praises to Jesus, to the Father, and to the Holy Spirit. Many such scriptures can be found in the Psalms, but you will find the whole Bible full of praise scriptures.

There's something about reading the Word aloud. It just seems to open the heart for worship. There are scriptures of thanksgiving, and scriptures of confession. I love them all.

This is the way my book is divided:

SECTION 1
> My personal needs
> My goals and dreams
> My family by name
>> With each name I claim a promise out of the Word just for them. I write their request, and from time to time ask them what they would like me to help them pray about. I love praying for their hopes and dreams. I feel as though I have a real share in their realized goals.

SECTION 2
> Fellow believers
>> This section is always a thrill as I write in the answers and see people that I love grow. I just smile and say to the Lord, "Look what we've done, Jesus."

SECTION 3
> My church
> The staff and their families
> The board
> The department leaders
> The Sunday School teachers
> Any special project that we're praying for
> Our adopted missionaries

SECTION 4
> My country
> Issues that concern me and my country

21

My president
My city
SECTION 5
The lost
My neighbors
Any special request made at Bible study

When you document answers to prayer, Satan cannot lie to you and say prayer is a waste of time. Prayer moves the mighty hand of God, and your prayer notebook becomes proof that this is true.

Here is a quiet time chart.

```
            Praise    |  Praise
            Listen    |  Confess
        Intercession  |  Pray the Word
        _____|_____
        Thanksgiving  |  Read
          Singing     |  Journal
```

My quiet time takes an hour, but you can modify yours for your personal time frame. One of the sweetest sections on the chart is the time allotted to singing. Keep a hymnal with your Bible and your notebook. Singing before the Lord is so cleansing to the spirit. It keeps you free in Him. When I sing or hear something sung early in the morning, it stays with me throughout the day.

Most people have forgotten how to be still and listen. Listening to the Lord is a most vital part of prayer. We generally have so much noise in our day that silence seems deafening. Listening opens our mind for receiving creative messages from the Lord. I love the passage that says; "Be still, and know that I am God" (Ps. 46:10).

As we grow in the Lord we will have a better understanding of what God is trying to teach us. The reason some Christians remain baby Christians all their lives is because they do not set aside a time each day to spend with the Lord. You never outgrow your need for a personal quiet time. There is no other way to gain a teachable spirit.

Here are some other ways to grow.

22

Hearing

When the Word of God is preached, we receive new insights from godly pastors. I take notes when a sermon is given. It helps me to listen and to retain. It is also a good study method for the week to go back over the scriptures and get them firmly in my mind. Good teaching is another form of hearing the Word. Our local church is blessed with good Sunday School teachers. My teacher, Dr. Jim Johnson, has been teaching a series on the home, and the lessons are full of scripture. I'm always learning from him. I thank God for Spirit-filled teachers.

Another tool for hearing is tapes. One of the nicest gifts I ever received was the New Testament on cassette tape. Hearing the Word read is such a marvelous way to be renewed. Many times I listen as I get dressed in the morning. It's wonderful to have a player in your car, so you can listen as you run errands or take trips. This is in addition to reading. Except in cases of vision problems, tapes should not take the place of your quiet time.

Reading

By reading the Word we become acquainted with our Heavenly Father. The Bible is His love letter to His children (you and me). Use a bold-type printed Bible, one with margins that you can write in. Underline and make some notes with dates. Gerald discovered a plan for reading the Bible through in one year; read three chapters a day and five on Sunday. I have a tendency to read in one book and study there for a year, but we do need an overview.

Journaling

By journaling I mean keeping a diary or notebook of quiet-time thoughts. This leads us into personal truths, and writing down what we read and hear helps us to retain what we have learned.

Hear it.
Read it.
Write it.
Tell it. And it's yours for keeps.

Memorizing

We may have convinced ourselves that we can't memorize. We look up a phone number and check it three or four times while we're dialing. We don't trust our memory. God gave us wonderful minds, but they must be used or they become rusty like an old piece of machinery.

I don't enjoy waiting on traffic lights or other places of short, unexpected stops. A good way for me to memorize is to have scripture written on little cards that I can keep in my purse. When I have to wait, I can work on my memory verses.

When Barbara Chaney's children were small, she would put a verse each week on the refrigerator, and during breakfast they would work on just that one verse, memorizing it as a family. Perhaps you could give yourself a little prize for memorizing a verse a week, like a new plant for your kitchen . . . I promise, Gerald, no more plants.

Meditation

Practice being still in the presence of God. Think on His goodness, His mercy, His understanding, His forgiveness, His love. I try to picture Jesus when He was here on earth. I paint pictures of Him in my mind; playing with the children, laughing with His men, being very gentle with the sinners and the sick in body. I love the verse, "Thou wilt keep him in perfect peace, whose mind is stayed on thee" (Isa. 26:3).

Our children's pastor, Dale Hardy, shared his method of quiet time with me. It works well for those who are willing to keep a journal.

Reflection

A view of the past 24 hours. Write down any area in which you haven't lived up to your ability. Enter any conflicts that might have occurred, temptation, or even sin. This is used as an accountability check.

Discovery

Read the Word until it speaks and then write it down. This covers two areas: What is my reaction? and, What will I do about what God has shown me?

Ministry

List prayer requests, number them, and add to your list all year, making note of answers and the date answered. Then ask God to give you instructions for ministering to someone that day.

The following pages are examples that you can use for your personal devotions and also share with your Bible study group. The one with three sections is very easy to use and can be used in a Bible study group as a starter method.

Write the passage	Paraphrase it	Apply it to you
_____	_____	_____
_____	_____	_____
_____	_____	_____
_____	_____	_____
_____	_____	_____
_____	_____	_____
_____	_____	_____
_____	_____	_____
_____	_____	_____
_____	_____	_____
_____	_____	_____
_____	_____	_____

If you use this chart for a beginning Bible study, perhaps you'll want to print the portion of scripture for that day. I saw this used at a large seminar to set the tone for the day, and it was a very special time of quietness for me, even with all the people around. After the study time we then shared in groups of three or four.

Along with the study portion you might also like to print some of these prayer list sheets just to teach your group how to do one for themselves.

IN	OUT	PERSON OR SUBJECT NEEDING PRAYER

If you fail to have your devotions one morning, you have not lost out with the Lord. Satan may put such a guilt trip on you that you feel like *such* a sinner. Remember—Jesus is your Friend and He's more interested in you making it than you can imagine. Mark off a spot and start over. The Lord must love new beginnings; he gave us Mondays, the first of every month, and each new year.

Please take the time occasionally to be still in the presence of Jesus. Stay until you are purged of any bad attitudes or hang-ups that would hinder your walk. We need to have the dry ground flooded every so often.

Our Jonathan has been such an individualist—so free and independent. When he was growing up, his attitude would sometimes get out of line. The Lord taught me that what he needed at that time was love expressed, so I would hug him close, tell him how precious he was, how gorgeous he was, and oh, how very much I loved him. Immediately he would respond with a new sweetness and openness in our relationship. One day I was standing at the stove fussing over something in my life. My attitude was anything but sweet, when Jonathan walked up behind me and said, "Mom, what you need is a big hug." It sweetened me for sure!

So it is with Jesus. Because He knows us so well and loves us so much, He knows when we need a big hug. It's usually when we've been naughty. Let Him hug you from time to time. It will change your life!

Allow the Lord to be your closest Friend. Such a relationship requires cultivation. You can't develop a friendship on the run. You must take the time to get to know Him.

Please do the Bible study that follows:

Bible Study

Personal Bible Study

1. I will _____ thee and _____ thee in the way which thou shalt _____: I will _____ thee with mine _____ *(Ps. 32:8).*

2. But as touching _____ _____ ye need

   not that I write unto _____: for ye yourselves are

   _____ of God to _____ _____

   _____ (1 Thess. 4:9).

3. _____ is the man whom thou

   _____, O Lord, and _____

   him out of thy _____ (Ps. 94:12).

4. Thus saith the Lord, thy Redeemer, the Holy One of Israel;

   I am the Lord thy God which _____ thee to

   _____, which _____ thee by the way

   that thou shouldest _____ (Isa. 48:17).

5. But the _____ which ye have

   _____ of him _____ in you, and ye

   need not that any man _____ you: but as the same

   _____ teacheth you of all things, and is

   _____, and is no _____, and even as it hath taught

   you, ye shall _____ _____ _____ (1 John 2:27).

6. He that _____ the heathen, shall not be

   _____? he that teacheth man

   _____, shall not he know? (Ps. 94:10).

7. Having then _____ differing according to the

   _____ that is given to us, whether

   _____, let us _____ according to

   the _____ of _____; or

   _____, let us wait on our ministering: or he

   that _____, on _____ (Rom.

   12:6-7).

8. Fear _____ not; for _____ am with _____: be not

   _____; for I am thy _____: I will _____

   thee; yea, I will _____ thee, with the _____

   hand of my _____ (Isa. 41:10).

27

9. But my _____ shall _____ all your _____
   according to _____ _____ in glory by
   _____ _____ *(Phil. 4:19).*
10. It is _____ in the _____. And they
    shall be all _____ of _____. Every man there-
    fore that hath _____, and hath _____ of
    the _____, cometh unto me *(John 6:45).*

4

Why Bother?

And whether one member suffer, all the members suffer
with it; or one member be honoured, all the members
rejoice with it. Now ye are the body of Christ, and members in particular.   *1 Cor. 12:26-27*

Not too many years ago, women lived in the
same place all their lives. They washed clothes together, they quilted
together, they had their babies together, and any time there was an
emergency they had each other, because they lived as a family community. There was a grandmother, mother, daughters, aunts, cousins.
I'm not very old and I remember when our family was like this.
Now we're so transient, we're scattered all over the globe. We've become isolated, locked into our little world. Women are lonely!

We expect our husbands to meet all our needs, and men just
aren't equipped to do this. Frankly, they aren't interested in all the
little details that women love. This is why I believe so strongly in
Bible studies for women. In Bible study a closeness is developed that
cannot be found anywhere else. To find a kindred spirit is so affirm-
ing. We discover that we're not weird; others are having the same
struggles. We're in this together.

When women come together and study the Word, they learn to
be honest and open. Small-group studies give us a vent for our emo-
tions in a safe climate, and other women to identify with. We have

29

role models who teach us through hard places that they are struggling with that we, too, can make it. By sharing the victories, we are taught how to rejoice as well as weep.

Some of my dearest friendships have come through Bible study. In a small group we come to depend on one another. We're challenged to meet needs and be dependable; this builds character. It's beautiful the way the Word binds us together. Often I've felt the women in our group, my dear friends, were my teachers, for they were. I learned by watching their lives how to love my family better, to be loyal and true, and always come away with a deep desire to be more Christlike. We are truly taught by one another!

One of the basic elements of a Bible study is that it teaches us to feel good about ourselves and who we are in Jesus. The world gives out messages such as "Unless you're a perfect size 10—unless you're a terrific sex partner—you just don't have it together." All day the world screams at women, and they begin to believe that they are in competition with all these things. We really need each other. Bible study with other women is an island of peace where we discover that we only have to be ourselves.

Paul wrote in Titus 2:1, "You must teach what is in accord with sound doctrine," and in verses 3-5 of that chapter, "Teach the older women to be reverent in the way they live, not to be slanderers or addicted to much wine, but to teach what is good. Then they can train the younger women to love their husbands and children, to be self-controlled and pure, to be busy at home, to be kind, and to be subject to their husbands, so that no one will malign the word of God" (NIV).

God wants us to have a teachable spirit. This is a must for Christian growth and development. He will teach the older women or those who have walked with Him longer, so that they in turn can teach the younger in years or faith. We learn so much from each other, but only with a teachable spirit can we receive what is being taught. The only way to develop a teachable spirit is through a life that is totally committed to Christ. We must become convinced that Jesus is "the way, the truth, and the life" (John 14:6), and "in him we live, and move, and have our being" (Acts 17:28). When we are convinced of this, we will want to transfer that concept to others. We'll want to share the joy. We're taught on our knees how to receive, and when we have been in His presence long enough for Him to change us, then we are prepared to share who we are in Jesus with others.

I believe in women's Bible studies more today than I did 10 years ago when we started, because everything around us is more hurried and pressured than ever. We really need that time together to be renewed in our mind and spirit. In a Bible study you pull away from the fast pace of the world. Together you sit down, you're quiet, and as you read the Word, find practical applications, and share what the Word is saying, you become equipped to live in this crazy world. Just to know that someone cares is soothing.

All Christians should be involved in Bible study, for in order to grow we must be learning. The collective mind is a beautiful thing. When people think that they have arrived spiritually and cloister themselves at home, there is a danger of spiritual pride. Some think to be saved is enough! But it is only the beginning of an exciting journey. We need accountability to other Christians. To come together in a small-group Bible study and share your thoughts, you must take the risk of your ideas being challenged. This teaches you to be transparent, and helps you grow in areas where you are unaware of need. This is so healthy.

But women are all different! Some just love being at home, doing their own little thing. Many women are roadrunners. Some love to visit other women, sipping tea and talking. Our goal is to see the value of giving up some of these favorite pastimes for something far better. Bible study and discussion of each other's ideas is challenging, fun, and worthwhile. We learn to think for ourselves, and as we study the Word, we find out what He's trying to say to us today. We need not be blown about by every wind of doctrine. We can know what we believe, and why.

I look at our women's Bible study as a blessed event. I am convinced that in my once-a-week Bible study I grow in every way. I'm changed by my friends, challenged and renewed, encouraged by the fact that they love me. I know that I belong—and that is very important! A sense of belonging increases my self-esteem. We never get so old or so learned or so spiritual that we don't need to belong.

The first Bible study that I ever attended was a vacation Bible school at the First Baptist Church in Americus, Ga. I was five years old. A nice lady who taught the class did a lot of innovative things; we sang little songs, colored, made things; we pledged allegiance to flags; we played games and had refreshments. It created a pleasant setting which prepared us for receiving the Word of God. We memorized a Bible verse, heard a Bible story, and we were taught, really taught.

I've never gotten away from the beauty of that experience. The teacher probably was not a special person. She was just a lady like you and me. But she was willing to pour herself into others.

This is what Bible study is really all about: the pouring of one person's life into others so that they can become more like Jesus.

We can get so lazy and so wrapped up in ourselves that we're not willing to extend our love, our time, our compassion, to anyone but our little closed family unit and our very own selves. But you see, that little girl who loved VBS has grown up and still has those same basic needs: a need for fellowship, for companionship, someone to love her, pray for and with her, teach her, cry with her, laugh with her. She still needs a place where she can just be herself. Women's Bible study is precious because it meets needs . . . my needs and yours. If any organization does not meet needs, it has no reason to exist. Bible study meets needs!

5

That First Bible Study

Ⓦe Started Small

That first day is still so vivid in my mind. There were four of us: Coelita, Almuth, Sherrie, and I. We felt a real need to study the Word; we had chatted on the phone and in the aisles of the church, but now we were finally together. The Word had drawn us.

In the beginning we weren't so concerned about others coming. Sure, we wanted them. But *we* were hungry, so we came. It's easy to get hung up on who can or will come and be defeated by fear that no one will. Better to press on with the ones you have! We had no idea what God would do with our little group; we were just being obedient.

Even if there are only two of you, get started. Don't wait for the perfect time. Procrastination could rob you of the joy of ever getting started. We are all so busy and our days are filled with interruptions, and even nice ones hinder us from doing more.

The Day to Meet

We chose Tuesday morning for our study because Tuesday was before the noise of the week could drown us out. No day will be perfect for everyone, so you must make a decision and stick with it. Just remember there are seven days and one will be just right for you.

We met once a week. Some groups meet semimonthly and some once a month, but we needed the weekly contact. Giving a morning out of your week can seem like such a big issue, but if you will give it, it's like tithing—God gives back the time when you need it most. Honestly, there have been times I felt like the clock stood still just for me. I got done what needed to be done. Think of this time as an investment in your spiritual growth. You take the time to go to the bank, the doctor, the dentist, and even the spa. This is the most marvelous investment you can make, and it's worth it!

What to Teach

God's Word must be the central theme of your meeting. Please teach the Word. We have many wonderful books available today, but none can take the place of the Word. We started with the Book of James, and we took it verse by verse. In the beginning we didn't know much, but we did know that the Holy Spirit is faithful to reveal Jesus to us when we honor the Word. The Bible is so alive, and as we studied, we discovered new life in us. God spoke to us through His Word. We were rebuked, reproved, encouraged, elated, brought low, challenged, inspired, strengthened—changed! Praise God for His Word!

There are many Bible study books available. I'm speaking of studies that take the Word by book or by subject. These sometimes have a teacher's and a student's guide, and are a great help when you're starting out.

I highly recommend the Beacon Small-Group Bible Studies published by Beacon Hill Press of Kansas City (Box 527, Kansas City, MO 64141). These come in separate workbooks covering individual or naturally grouped books from the Bible. In the front of each workbook are helps for making the study more interesting. All the writers are top-notch; you will find the studies to be excellent for your group. Most of the New Testament is now finished, and it won't be too much longer before the Old Testament studies come off the press.

Don't substitute a book on child care or marriage for the study of the Word. Women may be excited in the beginning, but only the Word will bind their hearts together. Recommend Christian books on these subjects for outside pleasure reading. They are valuable. But don't use your precious Word study time to teach them.

We are living in a day when everything is analyzed. I am not an expert on anything, so I have no advice on complex matters. All I know and want to know is Jesus. I have been helped by greater writers, but I have been changed by the Word, and so will you and your friends.

No Gossip Allowed

We never allowed our time together to become a gossip session. Fear of gossip keeps women away from small-group meetings. There are many ways to gossip: a look, body language, in the name of prayer—we know them all. And don't let your women talk about how bad their husbands are. Every group will have someone who feels she must vent her anger, and it's easy in a safe place to unload. To stop this problem, ask the woman to tell the group some positive things about her husband, and she'll begin to see him in a new light. Naturally there will be times of openly sharing personal burdens, but you can control this to a great degree.

Stay on Time

My wise husband, my adviser now for 25 years, said, "Start on time and end on time." Oh, that was hard, because people tend to come late. The baby was sick, someone had a flat, or they got locked out of the house—you name it, it happened. Gerald kept saying, "If no one is there but you, start." So I did and it worked. Not only did they arrive on time, they started coming early. Ending on time was another challenge. Women love to talk. Remember your commitment; *to study the Word.* Be kind but be firm, and bring it back into focus. There'll be some off-the-wall comments that you can't plug in. That's okay, don't try. A certain amount of chatter is relaxing and allows time for ideas on the subject to surface. Find ways to get back on track, or go on to the next subject.

Don't feel that you have to cover the whole chapter each time you meet. Stop, and pick up at that place the following week. Don't be in a hurry, for you'll have lots of time to finish. But don't drag it out to the point of boredom.

Take Charge

Don't let anyone dominate the study time. Strong personalities will come on strong. The teacher must be in control as well as be Spirit-controlled. Each individual is important, but more so is the collective group. We've all attended classes or meetings where one person talked all the time. This may spoil the session for others who have come to hear the teacher and get their own questions answered. The teacher, while sensitive of the need to share, must not allow one compulsive talker to take over.

It's a Bible Study—Not Church!

We wanted our Bible study to complement our local church so we served as an outreach group. We were not a Sunday School class or a prayer meeting group; we did not take the place of these valuable church meeting groups. A Bible study is sometimes used to launch a new church. If that is the ongoing purpose, the method is ideal. However, our purpose was to help the women of our church to become strong in the Lord and in His Word.

We didn't try to make Nazarenes out of neighborhood ladies who attended the study. In fact, we didn't talk about churches. We met as women who had many things in common, and studying the Word was the reason for our meeting. Many women noticed a marked difference in our commitment and consecrated living, so they would ask individuals questions about our church and what we believed. As a result, women were both saved and sanctified in our Bible study. Cherry Thomas, an antique dealer, was a double-sharp lady. She had preformed ideas about Nazarenes, and she wasn't sure she wanted to attend our study. But Donna said, "Cherry, you'll love our group, just come and see." After a few sessions she was weeping openly as the Spirit would bless us with His presence. We were studying about the Holy Spirit, and one morning Cherry indicated that she'd like to share something. "I have been so hungry to be cleansed by the Holy Spirit and filled with all the fullness of God," she said, "and while kneeling in my own home I surrendered and He came in." We all wept for joy and praised the Lord. What a glowing person she was! She has since gone to be with Jesus.

You don't have to sell your church. Just give people Jesus and His Word. I've found when Jesus is lifted up He draws people to himself. This is why it is vital that the leader be full of God and not self. The most important thing the Holy Spirit does is reveal Jesus in all His beauty.

Home Bible studies should come under the guidance of the pastor or director of women's ministries. Material to be taught should be cleared. While everything can't be monitored, if it's church sponsored, someone should have the final say as to what is taught and be available as sponsor and advisor for the group.

You know the saying, "The hand that rocks the cradle rules the world." Our Bible study became the catalyst for a real revival. Women of the Word have the power to change a church, a home, a community, and yes, the world!

Our goal was to allow everything to flow back into the church. Women from all denominations were welcome, but we were Nazarenes, and we naturally taught our own doctrine and ethics. We centered on Jesus, so all who came respected us. A group needs boundaries, but we don't have to be hard-nosed about it. We existed to complement, not compete with other churches.

Sometimes Problems Come

When problems came up we handled them on our knees. There were issues that had to be tackled head-on. A group heard about our sweet fellowship and decided to check us out. They felt we needed some changes. The Lord and I talked this over and came to the conclusion that He was in charge, and as the leader I was to look to Him always, and not at the problem. The passage "Be ye therefore wise as serpents, and harmless as doves" (Matt. 10:16), came to mind.

The moment of confrontation arrived. I was sweet but firm: This is who we are, you are welcome as long as you recognize this. Some stayed, some left, but we continued to grow.

Such problems are another ploy of Satan to make us give up and quit. Don't listen to him, listen only to Jesus! Don't try to understand everyone; just accept them in Jesus. He'll do any changing that is needed. What a relief! I don't have to hold up the world all by myself!

Where to Meet

In the beginning we met at our house. It was a cute little parsonage. We didn't have much, but I loved sharing our home with others, and the ladies knew they were welcome there. Some of them had marvelous homes and that was fine, but they needed a role model in me; someone to lead the way by saying, "Come and feel at home." It's not what you have, but your willingness to share it that counts. Cleaning house for them was fun. They liked my plants, thought my wallpaper looked like me, and didn't seem to notice the worn furniture. We loved just being together.

We started around our dining table, but soon we were filling all the spaces. What fun we had. We didn't set out to be big; we just grew under the guidance of the Holy Spirit, and so can you. Just start and let God give the increase. Should you get discouraged, remember it's His project. He'll see you through.

My life has changed because of that Bible study, for I have become strong in the Lord. It isn't because I'm smart or most favored, but because I have a teachable spirit. A teachable spirit is always growing, always being taught of the Lord and others. A teachable spirit never arrives or becomes an obnoxious authority.

O Jesus, keep me warm, willing, and teachable. I'm just Your child, and oh, how I long to be taught!

Checkpoint

At the close of your weekly session ask yourself these questions:
1. Was your study interesting, exciting today?
2. Were you enthusiastic?
3. Did you accomplish what you set out to do?
4. Did you keep everyone plugged in?
5. How would you rate your lead questions?
6. Can the women live out what you taught?
7. Did you answer all your questions?
8. Were you careful to include everyone?
9. Did a strong personality take over?
10. How did you handle any problems that occurred?
11. Were you kind?
12. How did they leave? Were you able to lift their sights? Were they encouraged?

As you inventory your effectiveness, you will become more confident in your teaching.

6

The Gentle Art of Leading Women

But I have prayed for thee, that thy faith fail not: and when thou art converted, strengthen thy brethren.

Luke 22:32

Who, Me?

Maybe you've dreamed of leading a Bible study, but because of fears you just haven't started. Let me encourage you to trust Jesus with your dreams. He can make you equal to the task.

The leader is an ordinary person with an extraordinary love for Jesus and women. You cannot be a recluse and be a leader of women. Women will respond to anyone who loves and accepts them.

For too long I didn't know who I was or what my purpose in the world was all about. But when Jesus became real to me, I knew I was loved and free to love others. Women need to see in their leader that freedom to love. Aren't we afraid of being rejected! We have a tendency to pull back. We can stand our ground in the world because we don't have to expose our inner self, but in a Bible study group we allow ourselves to know and to be known, and believe me that's scary.

You must be willing to be transparent. Your life must be so hidden in Jesus that you have nothing to hide from others. No one is required to expose her private life; just the same, your private life must measure up to your public life or your witness is nil.

Who knows all the answers? You do not need to pretend you do. It is so refreshing to hear a leader say, "I really don't know, but I'll try to find out for you."

Laughter is medicine for the soul. Learn to laugh at yourself and with others, and you'll rarely be laughed at. This week in Bible study we were having such a beautiful time together, one of those days when laughter just flowed. Someone said, "We must stop this laughing; Christians shouldn't have so much fun." Then we really cracked up. I just loved it!

People carry such heavy burdens that they need to be taught to laugh again. You can teach them—teach them that serving Jesus is really a lot of fun. Christians should be the happiest people in the world. Some people resist Bible studies because they think we get together and moan. We do cry! But we also laugh. Aren't you glad Christians are normal, balanced people?

I believe the most important quality for a Bible study leader is to love Jesus and others more than oneself. Love breeds oneness. It identifies with hurts as well as with joys. To love another soul prevents put-downs. It doesn't keep you from being human, it just allows you to see others through the eyes of the Lord.

Probably you've thought: I couldn't lead a group, I don't have a degree. Or people would expect me to know everything. What prevents us from greatness in the Kingdom is not what others think, but what we think of ourselves.

Pray until you know the Lord will do the teaching and you'll be His mouthpiece. You don't want to lecture anyway. Allow people to share and as you direct their thoughts back to the Word, they will see the direction in which you're headed. (Women are so smart!)

You've probably heard the story, but I'll tell you again: God made man, took one look at him, and said, "I can do better than that"; so He made woman. *What a creature!*

Women are super! Once you've decided to lead women; you'll become so challenged by their potential that you'll become a part of God's dream for them. They can be anything they dream. The sad part is that so few really know this. You can love them enough to help them see what they can be in Jesus.

You're a Daughter of the King

How sharp do you have to look? You may be poor as Job's turkey, but you can be clean, pressed, and smelling sweet. A leader says to other women, "Watch me and I'll show you the way." You don't have to have expensive clothes to look sharp. My mother always said, "If you have good shoes, and they are *shined,* you can wear a cotton dress and look like a million." (Today we might say "cute sandals from K-Mart.")

My dream for you is that you will know how truly beautiful you are. The Lord made you, a one-of-a-kind woman. We are originals, dear to our Lord. Not another woman in the world comes even close to being you. To know this eliminates the competition and the comparison. Being an original gives us identity. You can be described—you have long hair, you're bubbly, you're tall, you have gorgeous eyes, you have a mole on your cheek—whatever. No one but you can fill the bill for you!

To know who you are in Christ helps you to relax around others. Then the real you shines through. To be uptight brings bondage to our spirit. Believe that wonderful verse, "Ye shall know the truth, and the truth shall make you free" (John 8:32)! You're free to be you and I'm free to be me. We can please our Father by being the person He dreamed we could be.

Work Hard

"Study to shew thyself approved unto God, a workman that needeth not to be ashamed, rightly dividing the word of truth" (2 Tim. 2:15).

Be willing to study hard. Pore over the Word until you feel sure of your lessons. When we have studied and prepared our very best, the enemy will come in and say, "You won't remember that," or "No one is interested in what *you* have to say."

Satan's work is to defeat. My husband says the only power he has is the power we give him. Plead the blood of Jesus over your mind and then thank Him for the privilege of being His servant. God inhabits the praises of His people. So praise Him for what He'll do through you. The enemy will have to flee.

Reading is vital for a good leader. Read all the time so that you can share new insights with the group. Don't allow yourself to become stale and repeat the same old stories each time you meet. Reading will keep a fresh wind blowing through your head. Also you'll be able to cull out the books that would be harmful for new Christians as well as older ones. You'll always be recommending books for them to read, plus they'll ask, "What do you recommend for me to read?" A *Books and Bibles Catalog* is available from the Nazarene Publishing House, Box 527, Kansas City, MO 64141. NPH will also order books for you if they do not have the one you want in stock.

A teachable spirit is always learning from others. Make good books your good friends, but make the Word of God your best and dearest Friend. Read it, study it, memorize it, meditate upon it throughout your day. I love the chorus based on Ps. 119:11: "Thy Word have I hid in my heart / that I might not sin against Thee / that I might not sin, that I might not sin / Thy Word have I hid in my heart." Can you hear the melody?

Christian magazines on the market are another source of enrichment and learning. Read the newspaper and be up on what's going on around you. An interested person makes for an interesting leader.

As you grow you will want to increase your library. Some books that I recommend are the following:

A one-volume concordance such as *Young's Analytical Concordance*
A Bible dictionary
A Bible atlas
Beacon Bible Commentary
Beacon Bible Expositions
A study Bible such as: The Open Bible or Thompson Chain Reference (now available in NIV)
Various Bible translations (such as the *New International Version*, King James, *New American Standard Bible*)
Single commentaries (for the books being studied)

Your *Books and Bibles Catalog* will give you a wide choice of Bibles and study helps.

I know these will take time to accumulate, but start. Request a book for Christmas or your birthday, instead of perfume. Someone said if you would read in your chosen field for 30 minutes a day, in a few years you would become an expert. How about that—you and me experts! I know for a fact that the more you store in your mind, the more the Holy Spirit will bring to remembrance when you need it most. There have been times when I was teaching and truths would come out that I had learned or read years before and hadn't even thought about when preparing the lesson for that morning Bible study.

Just Be Yourself

After you've studied, relax and enjoy the group. If you feel nervous, tell them and ask someone to pray for you. To involve others in our task makes us partners. People identify with our humanity, not our perfection.

Another thing I've discovered: When I feel that I have failed, someone always says, "Oh, that was just for me this morning." Truly, the battle is the Lord's!

People are starving for someone to be genuinely interested in them. Get involved with your ladies. Learn their names. We use first names even for our older ladies and I'll tell you why: To be called by your given name makes you have identity, and also it makes you feel young. So if they don't object, use the older ladies' first names, too. Make them know you can't make it without them, because you can't.

As your group grows, and it will, you'll want to use name tags, but for now, write the names in your notebook and get addresses and phone numbers. Send little love notes. Phone various ones just to say, "I love you, and if you ever need me please feel free to call." As you get to know women individually you will know their gifts, and you'll be able to place them in areas of responsibility that they will enjoy. This prevents assignments that people come to hate.

Being a leader sometimes hurts. Ola told me something important in those beginning days. She said, "Darling, people will come with their hurts and heartaches. Love them, pray with them, but when they leave, shut the door and go on with your life. Your family needs you too."

Oh, what wise advice. It's not that you don't care, you just come to understand that you give those and all burdens to the Lord. You cannot solve people's problems; Jesus can. You just serve as the go-between.

For a long time I tried to carry everyone's problems around inside of me. This was defeating, because I began to resent their coming. You don't have to live with resentment, for you are free, free to release it all to the Lord, free to love. Don't let the devil make you feel guilty because you don't grieve all the time over even big concerns. You can be caring without being overwhelmed.

Chronic complainers tend to eat up time that you need to be giving to someone who truly has a need. You don't want to hurt anyone's feelings and you won't have to. Just be wise. Keep your eyes and ears open. You're one smart cookie!

43

I've seen children neglected because someone would call, never asking if you were busy, proceeding to talk nonstop without breathing between sentences. It is not rude to interrupt with "Honey, thanks for calling; would you mind if I call you later, I'm super busy right now." If you do this a few times the message will get across. If not, unplug the phone when it's family time. Believe me, it will keep the resentment from building in your own heart, and save your kids.

Be Affectionate

Be openly affectionate. Hugs, pats, kind words, and always lots of praise. When something good has happened draw attention to it. Even people who have a tendency to be cold respond to genuine warmth.

To be vulnerable leaves you open to acceptance or rejection. Don't be afraid to be this way. Let people know you: your weaknesses as well as strengths, your failures as well as your successes. You're a human being, not a deified saint. You're a Christian in the making; you have not arrived. Your freedom in this will help others to relax and be themselves. After all, we're making it together; and believe me, we do need each other! You need their love and support as much as they need yours. They cannot minister to you unless you become transparent about your needs.

One morning I went to Bible study quite burdened. I had such a spirit of heaviness. I thought, What am I going to do? The Lord said, "Tell them," so I did. I said, "Would you pray for me this morning, like right now?" On our knees we went! What a knitting together of our hearts! The glory of the Lord was ours that day for sure. You don't have to make it a confession session. Just be honest about your needs.

Remember that the hardest person to be is someone else, and the easiest is to be yourself. When you know God has given you the assignment, go for it. Study, pray, be yourself, believe in women, love them, let them love you, and you will have a wonderful time doing the will of the Lord, as a gentle leader of women.

Bible Study

The Gentle Art of Leading Women

1. Then will I _____ _____

44

thy ways; and _____ shall be

_____ unto thee (Ps. 51:13).

2. And moreover, because the _____ was wise,
he still _____ the people _____;
yea, he gave _____ _____, and sought out, and set
in _____ many proverbs (Eccles. 12:9).

3. And how I kept _____ _____ that was
_____ unto you, but have shewed you,
and have _____ you _____, and from
_____ to _____ (Acts 20:20).

4. Let him that is _____ in the _____
_____ unto him that
_____ in all good things (Gal. 6:6).

5. And they sent out unto him their _____
with the Herodians, saying, Master, we know that thou art
_____, and _____ the way of God in
_____, neither carest thou for any man: for thou
_____ not the _____ of men (Matt.
22:16).

6. For in that he _____ hath _____
being _____, he is able to succour them that
are _____ (Heb. 2:18).

7. The same came to Jesus by night, and said unto him,
Rabbi, we know that thou art a _____ come
from _____: for no _____ can do these
_____ that thou doest, except _____ be
with _____ (John 3:2).

8. Whereunto I am ordained a preacher, and an apostle, (I
speak the truth in Christ, and lie not;) a _____
of the _____ in _____ and
_____ (1 Tim. 2:7).

9. Thy _____ have I hid in _____ _____, that I
might not _____ against thee (Ps. 119:11).

10. And though the _____ give you the _____ of
_____, and the _____ of
_____, yet shall not thy
_____ be removed into a corner any more,
but thine _____ shall see thy _____: and
thine _____ shall hear a word behind thee, saying,
This is the _____, _____ ye in it, when ye _____
to the _____ _____, and when ye _____ to
the _____ (Isa. 30:20-21).

11. The _____ women likewise, that they be in
_____ as becometh _____, not
_____ _____, not given to much wine,
_____ of _____ _____ (Titus 2:3).

12. Go ____ therefore, and _____ all nations, baptizing
them in the _____ of the _____, and of the
_____, and of the _____ _____:
_____ them to observe all _____
whatsoever I have commanded you: and, lo, I am with you
alway, even unto the end of the _____. Amen (Matt.
28:19-20).

13. Whom we _____, warning _____ _____,
and _____ every man in all _____;
that we may present _____ _____ perfect in
_____ _____ (Col. 1:28).

14. But _____ thou the things which become
_____ _____ (Titus 2:1).

15. _____ us, that _____
_____ and _____
_____, we should live _____,
_____, and _____, in this
present world (Titus 2:12).

46

16. Let the _____ of _____ dwell in you
    _____ in all wisdom; _____ and
    _____ one another in _____
    and _____ and _____ _____,
    _____ with grace in your hearts to the
    _____ (Col. 3:16).

I trust that these scriptures help you to see the reason for teaching. I am amazed at the availability of the Holy Spirit. Remember it is God's work and He has promised to equip us. I believe!

7

Where to Meet

And daily in the temple, and in every house, they ceased
not to teach and preach Jesus Christ.   *Acts 5:42*

Where you have the Bible study is very impor-
tant. You don't have to have a big, fancy place, but it should be a place
of welcome, where people can be themselves and immediately feel
at home.

I prefer to meet in a home for the simple reason that it lends
itself to warmth and friendliness. Your unchurched friends will
more readily come to your home than to your church, at least in the
beginning, and new people in the church will feel drawn into closer
friendship.

We tried a lot of things in the ongoing of that first group. We
started by meeting at my house every week. This way everyone knew
the address and could tell anyone how to find it.

Later, we met each Tuesday for a month at one house and the
next month at another. We planned it in advance so people could
put on their calendar where Bible study would be held for those four
weeks. (In large cities a little map would help.)

My friend Judy said it was always a privilege to have the Bible
study in her home, and as she cleaned she would pray that the
women who came would be open to receive what the Holy Spirit
would teach that day. Judy's house always sparkled. She's that way
too, always so fresh and open. She loved strawberries and even now

when I see a strawberry, I think of Judy and whisper a prayer for her.

Going into various homes is so much fun, because you really get to know people. Women love seeing each others' homes. They get neat ideas for their own decorating, and enjoy comparing notes. The leader gets to learn what each woman likes, which is nice if you want to surprise them sometime with a little gift to brighten their day.

Make sure there is plenty of good light in the meeting room. Shadows may be good for atmosphere, but you can't study the Word in the dark.

Your furniture is not important. We sat on the floor, on dining chairs, the hearth—we didn't care; we were together and love is blind to the haves and have-nots.

Being in the home encourages those who are not such good housekeepers to work harder. You really have a discipling team in a Bible study group that extends to all the areas of our lives.

We always arrived a bit early because we enjoyed visiting. We shared recipes, brought everyone up to date on our kids, and we did a lot of hugging. So many of the women were hurting; we became a family to one another, reaching out, caring, and sharing. Train your ladies early to minister to one another. Just to know someone cares can keep a discouraged person from going under when everything else seems to be coming apart at the seams. Draw out the shy ones, the ones who prefer the corner rather than the center of the room. The teacher must take the lead in friendliness. Even when you don't feel it, do it!

That first Bible study was in an air force town where girls from all over the world met together. One of our goals was to disciple them so that when they left we could send them as missionaries to their next assignment. Every person was important, even those just passing through.

A home Bible study is more than just learning about the Bible. It's catching the spirit of one another. It's the love that we're all so hungry for. Inviting someone into your home is really saying, "I love you and want you to share the joy of Jesus where I live."

Remembering those early days of our Bible study, I think about our dog, Ada. She would get so excited on Tuesdays when the ladies would start arriving. She was my greeter. She loved coffee with cream and sugar and would beg to have the remains of anyone's cup.

Her funny antics often broke the ice. It is so easy just to weave who you are into the time together. Don't try to be anyone but yourself. People love it.

Ada was such an ugly dog. I would try to fix her up with bows and such, but she just had a strange shape. She's like some folks I know. They're just a certain way and they can't be changed even with bows. Going into homes helped us to accept one another. Some people would get it all together and others just couldn't. Everyone was loved the same. *What we have and what we can do is not who we are.* We are children of God, accepted in the beloved. This is so important to the Body of believers.

Plan your schedule at least six months in advance. If someone has to have surgery or be away, you can just switch houses for that month. We are creatures of habit, and it helps to have the location written down. Announce your meeting place on the bulletin board at the church, in adult Sunday School classrooms, and in the weekly church paper, if you have one. We have a weekly calendar on the back of our Sunday morning bulletin. Switching houses in the middle of the month is unwise unless it is an absolute emergency. Someone is sure to get lost! Continuity is vital to any group meeting.

Later you may need to go to the church in order to house all your ladies. You can try this to see if it works for your group. It didn't for us, and this fall we're going back into homes. I'm so excited about it, just because I like the closeness. We're planning to have six Bible studies in different areas of the city during the day, but our professional women who meet at night will still meet at the church because it's easier for them.

One thing I've learned is to keep reverse well greased. If one method doesn't work, throw it out and try something else. Methods aren't sacred. Your ladies are the most important thing to consider here. Meet their needs! And we all know that needs vary from place to place. Just as we are different according to our country, culture, or locale, so we differ from church to church. Be creative, willing to change, and quick to adapt to what is best for you.

Perhaps you'd like to meet at the same place every week, or even meet at a restaurant. One summer we took our group to the park. It was a nice change. The place need not keep you from having a beautiful Bible study. The enemy will try to convince you that you just can't have a Bible study now because the conditions aren't perfect. Don't allow him to rob you of the job that is yours for the taking. Be positive, be aggressive. Just do it. Have a home Bible study. You'll never regret it, honest!

We have sometimes called off weekly Bible study in the summer, but had a monthly luncheon just to keep in touch. It is difficult for mothers of school-age children to get sitters for the whole crew, plus this is the time many people take their vacations. There are reasons why you could call it off, but there are reasons to keep at least the core group going. You'll know your situation and be the best judge of the matter.

Refreshments

Women like having tea, coffee, or a cold drink in the beginning of the study time. Don't let refreshments become the focal point of the study. I've found that if you have food, women begin to compete to see who's the best cook. Eliminate that by only having something to drink. Occasionally you might have someone bring some cookies. We tried a once-a-month potluck salad luncheon that was fun. We even exchanged recipes.

Some groups like to go out for lunch. This is good as long as people can afford it. I found that this has a tendency to separate people rather than draw them together. You always have a group who can go and a group who can't. These latter women feel left out even though they may say they don't.

I know that it sounds crazy, but food can take over. Don't let the enemy get a foothold here. Just serve something to drink and you'll be safe.

Here are some of our recipes for mixes that keep a long time:

Russian Tea Mix
> 2 cups Tang (orange drink mix)
> ¾ cup instant tea
> 1½ cups sugar
> 1 tsp. cinnamon
> ½ tsp. ground cloves

Mix together; to serve add 2 rounded tsp. per cup hot water.

Instant Cocoa Mix
> 6 cups nonfat dry milk
> 16-oz jar nondairy creamer
> 2-lb. box Quik (instant chocolate mix)
> 1-lb. box powdered sugar

Mix above ingredients. To serve fill cup ⅓ to ½ full of mix and add boiling water.

Instant Coffee (regular and decaffeinated)

Tea Bags (herbal and regular)

Store your mixes in pretty jars that have a lid to seal and they keep fresh for months. All you have to do is heat a pot of water. Use disposable cups and paper napkins. Remember to keep things very simple.

Take up a little offering to cover the cost of the drinks and cups. If your group is large, maybe they would like to go together and purchase a pot that would serve 35 or so. You might even have someone donate one. I found mine at a garage sale for just a dollar. (Smile.)

During warm weather just serve a pitcher of iced tea, lemonade, and always ice water. When you have goodies, don't get out the plates. Always insist that it be finger food, for in the most polite company, finger food is accepted.

I can hear someone say, "All these things have nothing to do with the spiritual." Don't you believe it. Jesus ate and fellowshipped with the people He was teaching, and everything He did was a learning experience for them. We want to keep a balance in all that we do, so whatever you do, do it heartily as unto the Lord!

8

Prayer Time

Praying always with all prayer and supplication in the
Spirit, and watching thereunto with all perseverance and
supplication for all saints.   *Eph. 6:18*

Prayer time is such a beautiful part of Bible study,
and you can pray in so many ways. I love the simple prayers of the
new Christians. They sound like love songs.

We used to stand, hold hands, and pray. It was wonderful. Just
one problem—standing for long periods lends itself to locking your
knees for support. We would be deep in prayer when . . . *kerplunk* . . .
Cathy had fainted dead away. She was also pregnant when this happened! It was like an announcement. Locked knees and fainting go
together.

Here are some ways to vary your prayer time and keep it fresh.

Conversational Prayer

This is such an open way to pray. The leader introduces a subject,
then others pray for that request in sentence prayers, no one praying
more than a couple sentences. When that subject is exhausted, someone introduces another subject. The leader is free to close at any
point.

By using this method, you teach your ladies how easy it is to converse with God. He is our dearest Friend and very interested in talking with us.

Here is a little format for introducing subjects:

ACTS

Adoration or praise

Confession, faults (your own and confessions of praise)

Thanksgiving

Supplication or request

The first time I took part in this was under the direction of my good friend, Elizabeth List. What a blessed time we had in prayer! Even the very shy ones got involved.

Praying this way keeps people from thinking that only the seasoned saint knows how to pray.

Directed Prayer

My husband uses this method often in his Wednesday night Bible study. He will tell of the needs in a certain area and has someone pray in specifics. Then he will have someone pray for the Sunday services. After requests have been made known, another prays for the sick. On he goes until all matters seem to be covered and he feels clear. At that point he leads us in a prayer of praise.

This may seem a bit different and not as free as you'd like, but it avoids people praying around the world, not giving anyone else a chance to pray. People who aren't quite that pushy can be included.

Prayer Box

This is a ready-made ministry for someone. You wrap a shoe box in lovely paper, leaving a slit in the top. Before the study begins there's time to write your request on the papers provided. Then when it's time to pray, the prayer chairman shares the requests as she prays. Some are not to be read aloud, and we ask people to indicate that. She also reports on answers. Someone other than the leader has to keep this going. You have enough to keep up with. Our lady, Edythe, has a prayer group and they hold these prayer requests before the Lord all week. They are very careful never to discuss the requests with others outside the group.

A Prayer List

Encourage your ladies to keep a running prayer list and take time each week to bring it up to date. This is important to the support effort that you are building.

Prayer Partners

Let people choose a prayer partner in the group. Some may have three people, so everyone is included. Encourage the partners to call and pray over the phone together, pray at the same time each day in their own homes, and allow their prayer partners to come inside by being accountable to each other.

Prayer Chains

The chain doesn't have to have a lot of people; in fact, as you grow you will want to form several, having 6-12 people per chain. Each chain will have a chairman. The leader will call that chairman as emergencies arise or specific requests are called in. She in turn will call the next person, and so on until everyone is called. The last person calls the chairman, who then knows everyone is praying. Immediate prayer is necessary in many circumstances, and united prayer moves the hand of God!

Inner Circle

This is made up of the senior adults in the study group. They are the seasoned prayer warriors. Some are called to intercessory prayer, and oh, how we need that today! All the really hard problems go to this group. Sometime you can't tell any details, so just ask them to pray. They can and they will!

I know you'll pray kneeling, sitting, or standing. The position really doesn't matter. Just bathe everything in prayer. It's a must.

The prayer life of the leader should be evident to the group. How we need to avoid spiritual pride! But it is true that the greatest compliment a woman can be paid is for someone to say, "She's a real woman of prayer."

Keep your heart warmed through prayer. It will keep you going when you want to quit. It will be a constant cleansing for your attitudes. Talk everything over with Jesus. He really cares and understands!

9

The Nursery

But Jesus said, Suffer little children, and forbid them not,
to come unto me: for of such is the kingdom of heaven.

Matt. 19:14

Because you will minister to women of all ages, you will need to provide a nursery to which the young mothers can bring their little ones.

Set an age limit. We took children through age five. This is a challenge. They have to be separated because of the age difference. Have someone type up the nursery policy and post it so it can be easily read. We handed one to every mother, too. Don't assume that mothers know. Make sure they do. Don't let the list be long and tedious, but make it brief and to the point. Make it positive and not negative.

Sometimes a nursery is easy and sometimes it's a real burden. It's an area to be bathed in prayer. Perhaps you could use the church nursery and hire a lady to stay during the study time. Be careful about hiring teenagers except as helpers to an adult.

The nursery attendant is vital to your group. Women feel strongly about their children, so we must provide the best care possible. Perhaps a lady in your church would take this on as a ministry (oh, joy).

In the beginning we had a lady open her home to which the babies could be brought. Later we hired our church sitters and paid them by taking an offering each week. Those without babies always were liberal in their giving. We even tried charging so much per child. Believe me, we tried it all.

A funny thing happened once. A lady brought her children by, then proceeded to do her weekly shopping rather than coming to Bible study. You will encounter all types of people, so don't be surprised by what they do; just love them and pray that they'll *soon* get the light.

This incident sparked a ministry we started for our mothers. On Fridays we had Mother's Day Out. The women could bring their children to the church in the morning along with a sack lunch. Then for a small charge they would be cared for until mid-afternoon. This was a real bonus to moms who could never get away from their kids. You could even have lunch with big people . . . *goodie!*

It seems that a nursery can have problems quicker than any other area of your ministry, so stay on top of the situation; keep it staffed, clean, and just be aware.

My friend, Sharrold, supervises and staffs our nursery, and it leaves me free to teach. Pray and the Lord will give you someone who will consider this a real ministry.

10

From Bible Study to Women's Ministry

I firmly believe that the Bible study should be the foundation for a women's ministry; otherwise it becomes a social function just to give women something to do with their time. I love luncheons and retreats, but unless these flow out of a need to touch women for Jesus, they have no eternal value. I truly am bothered when I pick up a church paper and note a lot of information about all the projects and nothing mentioned about Bible study. Let's be in the Word more than we are in crafts and special projects!

When our Bible study outgrew the homes, we decided to take a long look at forming a women's ministry. This was years before we had any information from headquarters on how this was to be done, so we just did our own thing. Here are some of the steps we took. You may want to use them as guidelines.

1. Appoint a *women's director*.
2. She should choose a *steering committee* of around five ladies who have a vision and are willing to show up for work even when no one gets the credit. It helps to have gifted ladies, but basically you need positive, hard-working gals who love others more than themselves.
3. These six make up the dream team, and they should *meet several times* to pray together and share ideas until a purpose comes together. The first thing we did was choose a passage of scripture on

which to hang our purpose: "If ye abide in me, and my words abide in you, ye shall ask what ye will, and it shall be done unto you. Herein is my Father glorified, that ye bear much fruit; so shall ye be my disciples" (John 15:7-8). Our purpose became: to abide in the Vine, Jesus, so that we would produce much fruit. Our name became Vineyard. From there we proceeded to make our plans. Don't be afraid to think out loud. Write down ideas and toss things around until something gels. We asked the Lord to keep us from being sensitive about our ideas, so if someone shot them down it was really okay; we wouldn't take it personally. After we were established, we set a monthly meeting.

4. *Call a general meeting* of all interested ladies to share your ideas with them. Then ask for theirs. Write ideas on a flip chart or a chalkboard. Save the ones that will work, and be honest about the ones that won't. Tell them the committee will meet again, after which you will have another general meeting to bring them up to date.

5. *Put a brochure together.*
   NAME (We're called Vineyard)
   PURPOSE (To abide in the Vine, Jesus)
   COMMITTEE (Picture if you can afford it)
   SCHEDULE OF EVENTS (Or a calendar)

6. *Have a kickoff luncheon* and present your first women's ministry. Make it a celebration!

How We Started

We started with summer luncheons. We used a familiar format:

1. A theme
2. Special singer (two songs)
3. Special feature—Antiques, complexion-color-expert, family hairstyles, fashion show, etc.
4. Special speaker. We used our own ladies and asked them to include teaching the Word as they gave their testimonies or whatever the Lord had laid on their hearts. We used only women who were recognized as leaders. Too often we don't honor the special people right in our church family.
5. Special decorations. We gussied up that place. When the ladies arrived they were shocked. They didn't know we were so talented. We borrowed plants, candlesticks, flowers, antiques. You name it, we had it.

6. Hostess for each table. Her job was to make everyone feel comfortable and included in conversation.

We meet at the church, and the *steering committee* does most of the cooking with the *kitchen committee* handling the cleanup. The *decorating committee* makes it beautiful, and everyone pitches in and helps. We keep the menu simple and the price low.

The women love our luncheons and dress up for the occasion. We always schedule these for Saturday so everyone can come. Most men are home, so they take care of the children that day.

The Fall Session

We decided to use the quarter system and rotate the studies each quarter so the ladies could study three different subjects a year.

We have a time of welcome with name tags, coffee or tea available, and warm conversation. This we do in the foyer of the church. It takes about 15 minutes, never longer.

After the fellowship we go into the sanctuary, where music is being played. The *Bible study coordinator* is in charge of this portion. She brings greetings, shares any upcoming events, and sets the tone of the morning by her gracious spirit. We sing scripture songs, have our special time of prayer, with requests and praises for answers; most recently we had a 30-minute study on "God's Special Woman." At the close of this period we break into our small classes where the Bible studies are taught. We close promptly at 11:30 a.m. so the babies can be picked up on time. We encourage our girls not to dawdle. It is easy to spend 30 minutes just conversing while the nursery attendant is waiting.

We take an offering each week to offset the expense of the nursery, cups, coffee, etc. In the beginning we provided the books, but the expense was greater than our income. Ladies really don't mind paying for their own books. If you know someone can't afford a book, give it to her without any fuss so she won't be embarrassed. Often Cindy would make an appeal for funds if we were running low. People need to give; they are always blessed for it. It is the responsibility of the leaders to see that the money is used wisely.

In the summer before we started the fall session, Cindy, our Bible study coordinator, had several luncheons at her home to share the material that had been chosen to be taught. She encouraged us by the fact that she cared and she was praying for us individually. She made us feel that it was a high honor to be teaching a Bible study for Vineyard.

Our prayer chairman came early each Tuesday, along with many other ladies who gathered together and prayed for the morning session. Each teacher and all the activities were prayed for.

Before we began we sent out a feeler sheet for the ladies to check any areas in which they would be interested. We discovered lots of hidden talent. We tried to use women of all ages. Don't make the mistake of overlooking the strength of your older ladies. They really want and need to be used. They make marvelous greeters, teachers, prayer backers—you name it, they can do it. Use your young women for jobs that require lots of running, standing, and strength.

The Night Group

Women who work are often neglected. We think they're too tired to come out at night. If it's worth the trouble, they will come!

We used the same format at the night session as the morning with one exception: we did not break into small groups. The time was shorter, so we sang, prayed, had refreshments, and the teacher taught the study. We had about 50 women who came regularly. We touched lots of unchurched ladies with the night group.

We opened the nursery at night because we ministered to many single parents, and so will you. They need all the love and encouragement that we can give them. They are a vital part of our church. I guess I've learned more about compassion from singles than anyone else.

This was our time schedule:
Morning: 9:30—11:30
Evening: 7:00—8:30

In Addition

We sponsor many activities. The steering committee is responsible for planning these and executing the plans. Here are some of the things we did this past year:
A Valentine Banquet
Secret Pals
Mother-Daughter Tea
Annual Retreat for Women
Summer Monthly Luncheons

Couples' Night

    (We had pie after the revival service on Friday night.)

Christmas Kids

    (We adopted eight kids and bought toys, clothes, and food.)

Ideas

You can have a team that visits retirement homes to read, write letters, do hair or nails, or just visit lonely people.

You can have an arts and crafts fair. Have your crafty ladies make things and also invite local artists to take part. We charge so much per booth.

You can set up work teams to donate baby-sitting or house-cleaning for desperate gals—and we all have been there—during a birth, a death, or a sickness.

The ideas are unlimited. When neat women get together the ideas just flow.

Bible Study Groups

These are various-sized groups. Perhaps you'll find one that fits your needs.

Small Group   3-4 people

    1. Leader—a woman of the Word, warm and loving.

    2. An open home. Provide a well-lighted, friendly atmosphere and something to drink: coffee or tea.

    3. Be willing to invite others.

Medium Size Group   8-12 people

    1. A leader.

    2. A small committee to plan and dream.

    3. Coffee chairman (set up and clean up); also plan an occasional luncheon.

    4. Prayer chairman (form prayer chains and prayer partners).

Larger Group   15-30 people

    1. A leader.

    2. A steering committee (keep it small).

    3. Prayer chairman (form prayer chains and arrange prayer partners).

    4. Nursery chairman (secure attendants, pay attendants). This should be someone tuned into the nursery, perhaps a mother.

Largest Group   35 and more

This group will meet in the church or a large community room. Use a woman as a leader who is either appointed by the pastor or church board, or both. She should be a woman of prayer and the Word, with strong leadership ability, a person the women of the church look up to. She should look sharp and really be aware of the needs of the women she will lead. It is important that she have the gift of teaching. This is not so important with the smaller groups because they are primarily a share group.

Working with this leader there should be two other women to serve as an executive committee. These women will serve as coordinators, one over the teachers and assistants and one over the committee chairmen. These two ladies will free the hands of the leader in these areas, but it will be her responsibility to keep them encouraged and moving. They will be a dream team, a prayer cell, an inner circle. They have to work well together. This is rarely a problem, because women know how to communicate.

Cindy Speicher, the wife of our minister of music, Darwin Speicher, is our coordinator of teachers and Bible study materials. She has expressed her thoughts, which I want to share with you.

God is so good! He loves every one of us and wants us to become all that we can be. He wants us to become strong. Strong like a rock. "Strong enough to build a church upon," as our pastor would say.

Of course, He loves us even when we are not strong, even when we fail. He is always there to comfort and uplift us, putting us back on our feet, facing in His right direction. I am convinced that is why He gives us some of life's greatest thrills through challenges, helping us to stretch and exercise our spiritual muscles. Challenges motivate us to do better and in turn, motivate others to do and be better too. God, who knows all things, knows our limitations but has chosen us to carry out His work through Jesus Christ.

Becoming a successful coordinator is a challenge that is only possible through Jesus. I speak of success not in numbers but in true fruit from the Vine. Unless our motives for leaders and the Bible studies that are chosen are backed with prayer, the Word of God, and a personal daily relationship with Christ, the joy of sowing seeds will be drained from us and we will become doers of works.

When I was first asked to be the coordinator for Vineyard (our women's ministry), I was excited at the opportunity of working for Christ in this type of ministry. Later, however, was a different story. I began hearing a small, annoying voice asking me, "Do you really think you're going to be able to do this?" After all, I'd never done anything like this before. Who did I think I was, trying to choose leaders and Bible studies for all ages of women, in all stages of their spiritual lives?

I decided to ignore the voice and press on. What a challenge! I went to my Bible for assurance. Whenever I am faced with a challenge, I go to His Word for a scripture to plant my feet upon. As always, I was given the very thing I needed: "I can do all things through Christ which strengtheneth me" (Phil. 4:13). What a reminder! I would not be doing this alone. With that kind of assurance and Co-worker, what more could I need?

I began making out a list of possible leaders. I tried to think of anyone who had led or was leading a Bible study at the time, those I knew who were already grounded in the Word. I began to pray that God would lead me to the right women. I felt it was important that a possible leader have a burning desire to learn more about God's Word and an eagerness to share it with others. Most importantly, she had to be a mature and growing Christian. One of the requirements to being chosen as a teacher was to submit a handwritten testimony of her life with Jesus. This was put in our files. It helped me in seeing how very special and precious Jesus was in each one of their lives.

I then tried to think of anyone who might be interested in teaching. After I had come up with my tentative list, I shared the names with the other ladies on the steering committee. With some suggestions added, I was ready to start asking. But before I did I began praying over the list, praying for each name individually. I thought the list looked great, but I wanted God's approval.

With my list in front of me, I began making phone calls. Some said yes; some said no; some said they'd pray about it.

The list was relatively easy to make; why didn't I get better response? Within the next week, one by one, all but two ladies dropped out for one reason or another. I began backing up, remembering all that I had done. I had picked the most qualified ladies I could think of, used loving suggestions, even prayed over each one individually. I had decided they were the right ladies. What was wrong? I started hearing that same small, annoying voice, "You shouldn't be doing this. This job is for someone more qualified, more experienced. You haven't even started and already you're failing."

I chose to ignore it. I began to pray, remembering God's promise to me: "I can do all things through Christ which strengtheneth me." Whom had I forgotten or overlooked? "Lord, show me, lead me." I soon began to realize my decisions and God's decisions were not the same. We needed leaders, willing workers for the Kingdom. Where were they? Sharing this with some of my friends, to my amazement they were willing to serve, even excited! Right under my nose. Praise the Lord! All I needed was one more lady.

"Why don't you teach it, Cindy?" someone said.

"Me?"

I never even thought of that. Then I heard that voice say, "But you're so busy. You have choir, social commitments, two small children, you're even pregnant." That small, annoying voice had become a roaring lion. I chose to rebuke it in the name of Jesus. "I'll teach; I'll do it!" The last spot was filled! All the classes had leaders and assistants. Glory!

As I looked at my list, remembering how it had changed several times, I had a feeling of real joy and peace about each name on it. It was no longer my list, but God's. I knew He had chosen each lady (even me). What an assurance I had the first time I saw their beaming faces looking up at me in my living room, at our first leadership meeting! God is so good!

Our pastor, Gerald Woods, has a saying. It goes like this:

Work hard!
In all matters trust God;
Do the best you can,
And let the loose end drag.

I have tried to share with you how our leaders were chosen to encourage all those who may become coordinators. If you see some of my loose ends dragging, I'm sure as women you will find some way of tucking them in, sewing them up, or cutting them off. May God bless your efforts in building the Kingdom!

Cindy Speicher

We really expect a lot of our ladies. But you know, they come through. There are always some whose jobs prove to be unsuited to them. We try to make them feel wanted, but at the same time we find someone who can perform. There is never a place to quit when working with women. Hang in there! You can't sacrifice the whole plan for the sake of one person who can't or won't follow through. The following are some job descriptions. You will think of neat things to add.

FLOW CHART
FOR VINEYARD BIBLE STUDY
Director of Women's Ministry
(appointed by church board)

Committee coordinator	Bible study coordinator
Prayer chairman	Bible study teacher/assistant, Study No. 1
Nursery chairman	Bible study teacher/assistant, Study No. 2
Music chairman	Bible study teacher/assistant, Study No. 3
Coffee chairman	Bible study teacher/assistant, Study No. 4
Kitchen chairman	Bible study teacher/assistant, Study No. 5
Decorations chairman	Bible study teacher/assistant, Study No. 6
Luncheon chairman for summer	Coordinator is responsible for all material to be taught.
Retreat chairman	

Teachers and Assistants

A teacher must have a teachable spirit. She must be committed to the total dream for the Bible study. She must be able to share her faith openly and simply. A teacher must be loyal to the leader, so they may always present a united front.

The teacher is responsible for discipling her assistant, spending time each week in prayer and sharing what God is teaching her.

The assistant has to be willing to be second banana, submitting to the authority of her teacher and also the leader. She must be committed to spending the time to learn from her teacher. She must stay alert to the needs of the class so she can help keep the teacher informed of any changes. The assistant could phone absentees or send little love notes. She truly must be willing to be a helper wherever needed. She must have a servant's heart.

Coffee Chairman

Refreshments are used as a way to say, Hello, I'm glad you're here. Have a pretty table with something hot and perhaps something cold to drink. We made a pretty calico tablecloth. And we use the jars with the dried mix. (The recipes were given earlier.)

Welcome Chairman

This little gal is a winner, smiling and genuine. She makes the first impression for the group. She must be a lover of women. A card needs to be made out on each new lady, and then she should be given a name tag. Make the name large so it can be seen at a glance. This chairman keeps a file on everyone; she also is responsible for keeping all her material in a safe place. She, too, needs a helper. She should introduce all new ladies to others in the group.

Nursery Chairman

This is where we need prayerful consideration. The lady chosen for this ministry should be a mother, and she should understand the need for good nursery care. The chairman is responsible for hiring and firing. To have a nursery is like giving a mother a gift—two hours to talk and listen to big people. If you have problems in the nursery, it will affect the attendance of the Bible study. Stay informed as to needs. You will need to expand! The nursery will grow as the Bible study grows. We pay minimum wage. We pray often for this financial need.

Music Chairman

This should be a person who understands worship. You don't want a performer. Our lady uses scripture songs printed on an overhead projector and we sing along. She's always teaching us new ones. If she plays the piano, fine, but women's voices also sound beautiful without accompaniment. You can have printed music sheets, but looking up seems to help when you sing. Before long you will have the words memorized and can use them in your private worship time, as well.

Prayer Chairman

We have already covered most of the description of this chairman in previous material. She should be recognized as a woman of prayer, a person who would not feel put upon to carry prayer burdens. Encourage her to use innovative ways of prayer, such as sentence prayers, directed prayer, small-group prayers, or conversational prayer. She must be a woman who can keep confidences, for there will be many confidential prayer matters.

Kitchen Chairman

We have a chairman and a cochairman for this job. They come early on the day of the luncheon to help get the food out on time.

Afterward they have a crew of workers to clean up and put everything away that belongs to Vineyard. These women deserve a trophy for work done behind the scenes.

Decorations Chairman

Dotty is one of those creative people who can take trash and make it look like treasures. She is constantly adding to our collections of goodies. We have tablecloths made out of perma-press sheets. She had some ladies hem 45-inch squares of red and white checked gingham to use for an overlay. Sometimes she uses place mats and napkins to match, with napkin rings made from all manner of goods. She's lavish with her use of plants. She works long and hard and never complains. We all love to help her because we learn from her. She never tries to intimidate those of us who are all thumbs. This position should be filled by one willing to operate within the budget—a good shopper.

Retreat Chairman

The steering committee appointed Florene to this position, and she in turn appointed a board to assist her. They meet to discuss a place, a speaker, food, bed assignments, door prizes, music, afternoon activities, and the like. She is the one in charge, and the committee depends on her to finish what she has started. I read somewhere that a few people know how to delegate responsibility, and even fewer know how to delegate authority. This chairman must have the authority to do her job, otherwise the women's ministry director will be doing it all.

All of these assignments take watchcare and love. Please be willing to give people time to grow and learn. It takes years for a women's ministry to really gel. I've found that we are constantly changing things as we learn. As I've said before, keep your reverse gear well greased. Don't be afraid to say, "That didn't work but maybe this will."

Ruth Gibson in Kansas City has lots of wonderful ideas for women's ministry, and she would love to share them with you. Just address your inquiry to:

Ruth Gibson
6401 The Paseo
Kansas City, MO 64131

Also please refer to the workbook of ideas compiled by Berniece Garsee: *Program Handbook for Women's Ministries . . . You Asked for These!*

11

Who Will Come?

And, behold, a woman in the city, which was a sinner, when she knew that Jesus sat at meat in the Pharisee's house, brought an alabaster box of ointment, and stood at his feet behind him weeping, and began to wash his feet with tears, and did wipe them with the hairs of her head, and kissed his feet, and anointed them with the ointment.
Luke 7:37-38

When I close my eyes and see the parade of gorgeous women that God has sent my way, what a beautiful sight! How different they were, but all were very special, not only to me but especially to Jesus. There were times that I felt as though I had witnessed the wiping of Jesus' feet with their hair. What a fragrance! How precious to be taught the deep things of God by these babes in Christ!

Brenda

Jan said, "Come have lunch with our family today; I have a new friend for you to meet."

Their family pet had swallowed the squeaker out of a little toy and had to have surgery. The girl assisting the veterinarian had just moved to town, and Jan moved right into her life. During the surgery they talked. Jan said, "Come to our church with us tomorrow. I'll pick you up and then after church we'll have lunch together, and you can meet Pastor and Paulette." Since Brenda was alone and missed her family, she said, "Okay."

That's how it started. Then Brenda met Mike and they fell in love. They came to church together, and we watched their romance develop into a marriage.

Brenda didn't work after they were married, so she came to Tuesday morning Bible study. She was the one who came early and welcomed everyone. She washed cups or threw away the paper ones. She *never* missed. She was totally committed to Jesus. What a witness! She wasn't a leader, she was just Brenda. We all loved her deeply; she could always be counted on to do the job no one else wanted to do.

One summer afternoon she and her husband headed to Albuquerque and then on to Colorado for a vacation with her folks. A big truck with the driver asleep at the wheel hit them head-on, killing them instantly. I can hardly write this, for the pain of my loss is still sharp.

Brenda went to be with Jesus along with her precious Mike. We were all stunned and crushed. How could we manage without her? One soft, quiet girl—yet we were all changed by her presence at Tuesday Bible study.

So you see God has a place for us all. Brenda made Tuesday special for a lot of people, and she never taught . . . or did she?

Thanks, Jan, for bringing Brenda into my life.

Mary Jo

Never have I met a more fragmented person than Mary Jo. One of the girls in our Bible study invited her to come with her on Tuesdays. She looked like a frail, wounded little deer. She was pregnant and yet very thin. I was overwhelmed by the look in her huge eyes; there was such a raw need for love and acceptance.

Her husband was Jewish, but he didn't seem to mind her coming. For some reason I kept thinking, "He'll say she can't come anymore," because he was very jealous of her love for Jesus. He would say, "How can you love *Him* more than me?" She was able somehow to keep things balanced, and we all marveled at her strength.

I visited in their home many times. Sometimes he was warm and receptive; at other times he would be very cold. He would allow one to come only so close. I think he liked the difference that salvation made in Mary Jo, but was afraid for himself.

Little by little she told me her story. She was abused by her father and used as his wife from an early age. She hated him and had married to get away from home. Her sister had become a lesbian as a result of the abuse. What deep-seated pain! She needed so much love, and the girls at the Bible study just wrapped their arms of love around her.

She experienced such healing, everyone was amazed at her growth. She had come to know Jesus before coming into our group, but as a result of coming she was filled with the Spirit and totally committed to the Lord. She was so honest it made all of us do some soul-searching.

We shared her struggles and rejoiced in her victories. She never put her husband down. She believed the scripture "The unbelieving husband is sanctified by the wife" (1 Cor. 7:14).

Once he came for Mary Jo after Sunday School. The fellows encouraged him to stay for church and he did. There was just one little problem, he was barefoot. There he sat on the back row with his wife and his bare feet. Our class had so many street people at that time we just accepted him as a matter of course. The older saints— well, that was a different matter. But do you know our precious people overlooked the bare feet and saw the man. He didn't respond, but Mary Jo certainly did. She was proud as punch that he came and that her church family loved him.

Love is so amazing. Oh, how God loves you and me! His love reached out to that Jewish man because his precious little wife came to a Bible study. She really became Jesus to him. She was always so patient; in my humanity there were times I wanted to write him off, but just like Jesus, she never gave up.

Oh, please, Jesus, help me never to give up on people that You have died for. Because You love me—love others through me.

Sheila

I'm sure you've met people you knew could take charge. Sheila could handle anything and anyone. There was just one problem: She couldn't handle her own life. She had made a real mess of things. She had the American dream: a successful husband, a beautiful home, and a darling little boy, but Jesus was totally out of the picture. One day she was sitting in her living room in California and out of the blue she decided she couldn't stay there any longer. So she took her hot curlers, her car, and left, not even looking back.

Lanny was a biker, drifting with the tide. Somehow he and Sheila started living together. A neighbor who loved Jesus invited them to a revival service. They went, and during the course of the week they were both wonderfully saved. Now what? They moved into separate bedrooms, and one night they were talking across the hall. "What about that marijuana?" So up they got and fed the garbage disposal a kilo of the weed. Sheila said, "We killed the Kitchen Aid disposal."

They were baptized and married. Lanny decided they should move back to New Mexico near his folks and really start over. This is where I met them.

Sheila went to work at the Retirement Ranch and there was Lila. Right away she invited Sheila to come and be a part of our exciting church. Our people loved them and accepted them, asking no questions. Sheila was gloriously sanctified, and what a radiant Christian! With that strong will yielded to God she put herself at His disposal.

After the baby arrived, she became active in the Bible study. We all adored her because she was so open and honest, plus she loved us.

As a young girl she had enrolled herself in a parochial school, for as she put it, "I needed the discipline and I didn't get it at home." As a result of this discipline, after being saved she became a real student of the Word, maturing before our eyes. I encouraged her to team teach with me, and she did. With precious tears streaming down her face, she encouraged those girls to pay the price and go with Jesus before Satan could wreck their lives.

We often wept together over the past and the deep hurt she felt as a result of losing her son. Sin leaves such scars. The joy of the Lord was her strength, and oh, how she leaned on Him!

Sheila developed a prayer ministry in our church with prayer partners and prayer chains that prayed through many a Saturday night. Many victorious Sundays were the result of those all nights of prayer.

Sheila is a beautiful miracle and part of my dream for women—strong in the Lord and in His Word. I wish you could know her; tall, and so pretty, with eyes that never exclude anyone. Jesus changed her and the Bible study helped to make her strong.

Ute

Out of the corner of my eye I saw her come into the room where we were taking art lessons. You could feel her presence, she was so alive! Dressed in beautiful European clothes, blonde and gorgeous, she moved into my life. Usually pretty people intimidate me, but not Ute. I felt drawn to this beautiful lady and wanted to know her. I heard her talking with some of the girls from our church. They were inviting her to come play volleyball with our Sunday School class on Saturday night. Well, she came, dressed in a delightful volleyball outfit. I didn't know they were even available. We were dressed in grubbies, but this didn't matter to Ute. She seemed to accept everyone; she was free and open.

She had been in America less than a month, and although she is German, she speaks several languages. We were soon chatting like old friends. During the course of the evening I invited her to come to Sunday School the next morning. She said she would like to, but her husband was playing tennis and she probably should go with him. He spoke up and said, "Oh sure, she can come. I'll drop her off before I go to the tournament." I remembered him saying, "She needs friends." So she came.

She was alert to all that was going on around her, and from the start she had a teachable spirit. She had been raised as a Catholic and didn't always know what to do with our open way of sharing Jesus.

Several of the couples adopted her immediately. They began to drop by to see her in her home and invited her to their homes. She was alone a lot because of Manny's schedule. Along with working for the air force, he was the tennis pro at the country club. She came to Sunday School quite often and finally came to a worship service. That happened to be the Sunday before Thanksgiving, and my husband talked about America being the greatest country in the world, etc., etc.! Well, she didn't take to him and she said so. I saw her in class the following week and I said, "Say, how did you like church this past Sunday?"

"Well," she said, "I love your church school, but your mass blew my mind."

I thought she wouldn't come back, and I was sad. I called her home after a few days and her husband said, "Oh, she went to Germany for a month."

Finally she returned and I went to call on her. She was still open, so I invited her to come to class the next day, and she said she would, but not to church. I said, "That's okay, Ute, we love you and just want to be your friend." So she came. When it was time to go to the worship service, she said, "I think I'll go with you." That morning she gave her heart to Jesus.

We gave her an English Bible, but she said, "Do you think I could get a Bible in German?" I said, "Sure," and sought out my friend Tom, who was a Gideon. Very soon she had her own Bible.

She came to Bible study every Tuesday with her German Bible, but being a new Christian she didn't know the Old Testament from the New. And we were no help because we couldn't read German! Donna had taken some German in high school, so she made it her job to figure out how the books were arranged in order to help Ute find the passages where we were reading. Ute was a quick student, and she grew by leaps and bounds—so very precious in the Lord.

She also attended the couples' nighttime Bible study, and I'll never forget one of her first testimonies: "I've only been drunk three times since I've been a Christian." It was very quiet in the den that night, but no one judged her, for we all knew she came from a culture that drank wine or beer with every meal. We just said, "That's great, Ute, you hang in there; you're really growing." And she was, perhaps not by our standards, but according to all the light she had. It wasn't long before she could find Titus without help from Donna. And it wasn't long until she was bringing her friends to Bible study and witnessing to her folks by mail. The Lord did the teaching; we did the loving.

That was six years ago. Recently when we were in Germany, Ute happened to be there visiting her family. We were fortunate enough to see her again. You should meet her, still gorgeous, but with a new beauty that only Jesus can give. She is so firm in her faith today, and it is because she was invited by some great little gals to come share the joy.

You talk about exciting—from the simple beginning of four ladies around a dining room table, to this—a woman, strong in the Lord. *Thank You, Jesus, for allowing me to be a part of that dream!*

Recently I received a letter from Ute. She now lives with her air force husband and family in Spain. She wrote that she missed her Christian community and is going to start a little Bible study for her neighborhood. Only Jesus can do this! And He uses women like you and me with a teachable spirit.

12

Jana

Jana is a little four-year-old. She's a preacher's kid, like me, and she gets hand-me-down clothes. Recently we were visiting in her home. A friend had given her two adorable dresses. Her big sister was trying them on her, and suddenly Gina said, "They're too short; you can't wear them."

I was watching and said, "Sure she can, she just needs a pair of leotards." Jana, who never cries, began to wail. I was bewildered. "Why is she crying?"

Gina said, "She doesn't have a pair of leotards."

How often have I cried and cried because even though I had many other things, I lacked what I needed. Somehow we long for the complete, instead of seeing what we already have. We miss the good by grieving over the bad.

It seems in my life I've always lacked a pair of leotards. Jesus is teaching me to use what I have. He's in the business of making much out of little.

I really wanted to do something great for God, but I always felt I lacked the one thing to make it complete. Then I read Col. 2:9-10: "For in him dwelleth all the fulness of the Godhead bodily. And ye are complete in him, which is the head of all principality and power."

You really do have it all together. Stop worrying about what you don't have and go to work on what you do have. Jesus will make you complete.

In finishing this book I feel it lacks something—*you*. You will complete it when you share a part of it with someone else, and they will continue the dream of women, strong in the Lord and in His Word. Because we are beautiful women with . . .

"a teachable spirit."